THE END
OF
TECH COMPANIES

ROB THOMAS

ALSO BY ROB THOMAS

Big Data Revolution: What farmers, doctors, and insurance agents teach us about discovering big data patterns

In memory of Joe Schutzman, who lived by the code, "Do right, fear nothing."

CONTENTS

Part IV: The Maker Era

FOREWORD

Over half a decade ago, IBM Watson technology was being taught how to play the Q&A trivia game show "Jeopardy!" At that time, it could sort through 200 million pages of data and return an answer in 3 seconds or less. It was the ability to never stop learning that helped Watson beat two of the game's most dominant champions. Of course, since then, Watson has been used to improve the odds against cancer, offer bespoke concierge services for travelers, for banking and retail, and to help us understand how children learn. It even went to Hollywood to study the movie trailer business (check out the trailer for "Morgan"). But there's a bigger point that shouldn't be lost here – Watson's cognitive brain is disruptive to all industries.

Although the author is a thought leader and one of the most dynamic executives at IBM – *The End of Tech Companies is not an IBM book*. However, be assured that the experiences, mechanics, strategies, and cautionary information that are covered in this book are truly market tested – the book is a collection of real experiences, both good and bad, that were acquired in an ever-changing market.

I've come to know the author of this vibrant and informative book both professionally and personally over the last five years. He is an unapologetically "addicted learner" and a relentless improver. Sometimes I wonder whether Rob is actually racing with Watson to see how much he can learn each day. Once thing is certain: you'll reap many benefits from reading this book.

As someone with executive responsibilities for thousands of employees and a mentor to hundreds of them, a Board member at Women 2.0 (a for-profit corporation that is focused on the advancement of women in technology), and an advisory Board member for the Queen's University Masters of Management Analytics program, I can't think of a trait that is a greater predictor of success than an unquenchable thirst for learning. This book should be required reading for any learner who wants to be relevant in today's economy, no matter what the industry.

Rob Thomas is known as a remarkable storyteller, and this trait is apparent throughout the book. Fronting the main themes are interesting factual stories with specific relevance to each chapter. If you ever have the opportunity to hear Rob present, you'll be treated to fascinating stories such as how Porsche rose to its iconic status, or the operational aspects of Tabasco hot sauce and how every batch looks the same because of the simplest of ideas, and countless other stories that relate to business. This book is no exception. (*Spoiler alert*: It starts with a story about US dominance in the whaling industry, and how that dominance subsequently disintegrated because the industry became irrelevant. Think of that industry as a tech industry, because that's what it was – in the 1800s.)

The End of Tech Companies is about extinction and its avoidance. You'll learn about the "macro shocks" that affect all economic constituents. This book provides you with strategies to not just "cope" with this massive transformation of our economies but to lead in it. For example, the advent of blockchain technologies is set to make extinct the business of house title insurance and third-party pay trust agents (among others) while at the same time bringing over 2 billion new entrants to the global economy with its distributed trust ledger. Are you one of those individuals who are resistant to the use of the cloud for banking? *News alert*: This is where trust will be stored in the future.

Feeling overwhelmed? Not to worry! *The End of Tech Companies* gives us a framework for how to sense, pivot, and thrive. This book is a fast, eye opening, fascinating, and empowering read. The book is a tremendous opportunity for personal growth and reflection – you emerge not only understanding why we are at the doorstep of "The End of

Tech Companies", but also how you can leverage it professionally and benefit from it personally.

In exchange for the small amount of time that you will invest in reading this book (whose entire proceeds will go to a great cause), *The End of Tech Companies* is sure to pay off from a self-learning perspective: It certainly did for me. In fact, I'm so confident about this, that if you're not satisfied, I will personally refund your money and make the donation myself.

This book empowers you to be change agent. No matter what you do, the knowledge that you gain will help you to act like a "thermostat", adjusting resource flow to maintain optimal conditions – not a "thermometer" that simply reports the temperature.

I apply a personal "Waste of time?" algorithm to everything I do – there are only so many hours in a day and quite frankly, I need more. I use this algorithm to see whether an activity I spent time on was a waste of time. The algorithm is shockingly simple: Was I smarter at the end of the activity than when I started it? Sadly, there are countless emails, meetings, and things to read that fail this test. For a lifelong learner, that's the goal: that you leave the "room" smarter than when you came in.

I hope you enjoy getting smarter as much as I did…

Paul Zikopoulos - @BigData_paulz

INTRODUCTION

"If you aren't genuinely pained by the risk involved in your strategic choices, it's not much of a strategy." –Reed Hastings

In the late 1800's, the United States was the dominant presence in the whaling industry. At $10 million—more than $20 billion in today's dollars—it was the fifth largest sector of the US economy. Whales provided a source of energy (oil for lamps) and the basis for a number of luxuries (perfumes, umbrellas, etc.). Centered in Massachusetts, the industry was a major driver of employment and productivity.

The US's dominance in whaling was largely due to innovation—larger and faster ships, better harpoons, improved winch technology for hoisting sails, and better compensation. The latter two innovations were especially interesting. The winch technology reduced the need for manpower on ships. Fewer sailors led to more profits and productivity. And the industry's compensation model was one of the first true innovations in pay. Instead of an hourly or daily wage, the sailors were paid a percentage of what they brought back to shore. A true alignment of interests driving higher productivity.

Despite all of this momentum and innovation, the whaling industry crashed in the 1850's and never recovered. As Derek Thompson points out in his 2012 article in *The Atlantic*, wages increased rapidly, providing an opportunity for other countries to enter the market. Those other countries adopted the technology and innovation developed in the United States, and with lower wages, were quickly much more productive. As wages went up in the United States, capital started flowing to new sectors, in particular the new sectors of the Industrial Revolution. Thompson summarizes it best, "It's about how technology replaces workers and enriches workers, how rising wages benefit us and challenge companies, and how opportunity costs influence investors and change economies."

The world economy is driven by innovation and productivity, and business models built for a previous era deliver neither. The model for whaling was built around new innovations, low wages, and a market with few alternatives. (Petroleum was not yet widely available as a substitute.) When those factors began to change, the industry quickly lost relevance and its leaders did not adjust quickly enough. Capital fled, and in this case, the industry essentially evaporated. The parallels in today's world economy are scary, but represent opportunity as well.

Business models that rely on traditional distribution models, large dollar transactions, and human-intensive operations will remain under pressure. Although this movement has been underway for some time, it is just now becoming more acute and starting to show up in the financials of the non-tech elite (i.e., business capital spending has been negative in 4 of the last 5 quarters as of Q3 2016). The non-tech elite have yet to embrace the fact that companies and tech companies are becoming synonymous.

Many "non-tech companies" tell me, "thank goodness that is not the business we are in" or "technology changes too fast, I'm glad we are in a more traditional space". These are false hopes. A fundamental shift is coming (or has already come) to every business and every industry, in every part of the world. It does not matter if you are a retailer, a manufacturer, a healthcare provider, an agricultural producer, or a pharma company. *Your traditional distribution model, operational mechanics, and method of value creation will change in the next 5 years; you will either lead or be left behind.*

It has been said that we sit on the cusp of the next Industrial Revolution. Data, Internet of Things (IoT), and software are replacing industrialization as the driving force of productivity and change. Look no further than the public markets; the 5 largest companies in the world by value are:

Apple -	$583 billion
Alphabet -	$545 billion
Microsoft -	$449 billion
Facebook -	$376 billion
Amazon-	$371 billion

As Benedict Evans observed, "It is easier for software to enter other industries than for other industries to hire software people." In the same vein, Naval Ravikant commented, "Competing without software is like competing without electricity." The rise of the Data Era, coupled with software and connected device sprawl, creates an opportunity for some companies to outperform others. Those who figure out how to apply this advantage will drive unprecedented wealth creation and comprise the new S&P 500.

Survival for the next 5-10 years requires that every company in any industry embrace its future in the tech elite to remain competitive. The fickle nature of the S&P 500 should not be understated. On average, 22 companies are added or removed from the S&P 500 every year. This number will double over the next decade, with 50-100 companies added or removed each year.

"If you aren't genuinely pained by the risk involved in your strategic choices, it's not much of a strategy." is what Reed Hastings said. He lived through this personally, when he moved Netflix from traditional distribution (DVDs by mail) to digital distribution (streaming). It was gut-wrenching, and many people doubted their ability to make the shift. Every company will make a similar gut-wrenching decision in the next 5 years.

This is the end of "tech companies". The era of tech companies is over. There are now only companies steeped in technology that will survive.

PROLOGUE

Warren Buffet built a track record as the world's greatest investor, delivering compounded returns of 21% per year over a period of 50+ years. Although there is much to learn about his approach to investing, the intersection of his business thinking and investment thinking is most interesting. Buffett pays careful attention to capital utilized by a business. Specifically, he believes the optimal business delivers high returns on invested capital, *while* requiring minimal capital. There is no better example than See's Candy.

As Buffett writes in his 2007 Annual Report:

We bought See's for $25 million when its sales were $30 million and pre-tax earnings were less than $5 million. The capital then required to conduct the business was $8 million.

Last year See's sales were $383 million, and pre-tax profits were $82 million. The capital now required to run the business is $40 million. This means we have had to reinvest only $32 million since 1972 to handle the modest physical growth – and somewhat immodest financial growth – of the business. In the meantime pre-tax earnings have totaled $1.35 billion.

In short, See's Candy invested an incremental $32 million over the life of the business, which produced an additional $1.35 billion of profit over that time, an unusually high return on capital. Typically, to increase earnings at this rate would require 10-15x that much capital. In this case, that was not required because See's product was primarily sold for cash (limited receivables) and the production/distribution cycle was short (minimizing inventory). These factors, and the limited capital required, make this is an optimal business in Buffett's eyes.

Although businesses that optimize capital have always been attractive, the traditional definition of capital has always focused on cash needed to run and finance the business. In the post-tech world, the playing field is leveled for many forms of traditional capital. IT equipment, software, or even something like logistics can now be acquired via cloud in a capital-optimized way. But, what if the definition of capital changes? What if The End of Tech Companies requires a new way of thinking about capital optimization?

The End of Tech Companies calls for a new lens to assess the relative competitiveness of enterprises. In fact, for many leaders in the post-tech world, employees (humans) become one of the main sources, if not the main source, of productive capital. Human capital must be optimized for productivity, to lead in this new era.

The analysis begins with a sampling of modern "tech companies". For consistency, any company with a large portion of services or consulting revenue is removed, because such companies tend to make the relative comparison less meaningful. To assess the productivity of the companies requires an analysis of enterprise value and revenue, relative to the number of employees. Here is the raw data:

	Employees	Enterprise Value	EV/Employee	Revenue	Revenue/Employee
Adobe	13,893	47,000,000,000	$3,382,999	$5,800,000,000	$417,476.43
LinkedIN	9,732	16,000,000,000	$1,644,061	$3,726,000,000	$382,860.67
Workday	4,900	14,200,000,000	$2,897,959	$1,549,000,000	$316,122.45
ServiceNow	3,991	12,300,000,000	$3,081,934	$1,367,000,000	$342,520.67
NetSuite	4,603	6,300,000,000	$1,368,673	$967,000,000	$210,080.38
Tableau	3,168	3,200,000,000	$1,010,101	$850,000,000	$268,308.08
Box	1,370	1,500,000,000	$1,094,891	$393,000,000	$286,861.31
Amazon	230,800	3.3E+11	$1,429,809	$134,143,000,000	$581,208.84
Apple	110,000	5.36E+11	$4,872,727	$213,651,000,000	$1,942,281.82
Facebook	13,598	3.15E+11	$23,165,171	$26,000,000,000	$1,912,045.89
Google	64,115	4.24E+11	$6,613,117	$87,000,000,000	$1,356,936.75
SAP	78,230	96,000,000,000	$1,227,151	$24,895,000,000	$318,228.30
IBM	377,757	1.72E+11	$455,319	$79,000,000,000	$209,129.15
MSFT	118,000	3.38E+11	$2,864,407	$92,664,000,000	$785,288.14
Oracle	132,000	1.54E+11	$1,166,667	$37,324,000,000	$282,757.58
Cisco	71,883	1.53E+11	$2,128,459	$49,161,000,000	$683,903.01
Intel	106,700	1.64E+11	$1,537,020	$55,355,000,000	$518,791.00

There are certainly some stark differences. The relative comparisons of NetSuite, Workday, Box, and ServiceNow are probably less relevant, given their SaaS business models, which are valued more on bookings, lifetime value, and customer acquisitions costs. A graphical representation makes it easier to see the relative positions of the companies:

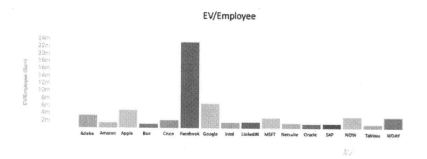

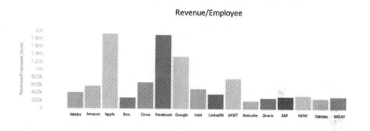

The difference in productivity is evident. An enterprise value per employee >$2.5 million is impressive. It is an indicator of above average productivity, driving expectations of future performance. Revenue per employee >$500,000 is also striking. It demonstrates leverage in the business model, leading to high productivity. The companies that exceed one of these metrics are solid. The companies that exceed *both* are truly leaders in the post-tech world.

For comparison, let's shift to a list of companies that many would consider to be the non-tech elite; companies that are leaders in their respective industries.

Company	Employees	Enterprise Value	EV/Employee	Revenue	Revenue/Employee
Caterpillar	114,233	$81,260,000,000	$711,353	$39,990,000,000	$350,074
John Deere	67,000	$60,990,000,000	$910,299	$26,730,000,000	$398,955
Nike	62,600	$84,000,000,000	$1,341,853	$33,000,000,000	$527,157
Coca Cola	130,600	$203,790,000,000	$1,560,413	$42,450,000,000	$325,038
Amex	54,000	$81,830,000,000	$1,515,370	$30,530,000,000	$565,370
Boeing	161,400	$89,000,000,000	$551,425	$94,860,000,000	$587,732
GE	333,000	$398,770,000,000	$1,197,508	$123,160,000,000	$369,850

None of them exceed the $2.5 million metric in enterprise value per employee. In fact, none exceed $1.6 million. In some cases (half of this sample of companies), a revenue per employee of $500,000 is achieved. Most poignantly, none of these companies exceeds both metrics, which indicates that they might be left behind in the post-tech world.

In the post-tech world, the primary capital deployed by any business is people. Although See's Candies might be the bellwether for great returns on capital in the previous era, it is companies like Facebook, Apple, and Google that dominate the post-tech world. But, even more striking is the gap that exists between those leaders and the non-tech elite, like Caterpillar, Nike, and Coca Cola. As mentioned previously, many among the non-tech elite are dependent on traditional distribution models, large dollar transactions, and human-intensive operations. The non-tech elite will quickly become non-elite, unless they embrace The End of Tech Companies.

PART I: MACROSHOCKS

There are four macroshocks, all occurring at the same time, that are expediting The End of Tech Companies, and ushering in an era in which tech is the default for all companies. These market forces are creating a sense of urgency, and companies will be compelled to act quickly or be left behind. It is quite possible that the next 36 months will determine which companies can evolve to the post-tech world. The losers might not be obvious after 36 months, but their fates will be sealed.

Chapter 1: Digital Transformation

"How many industries are left, where if you digitize some existing component of it, you introduce network effects in a way that was unanticipated, and leads to the potential for exponential growth?" –Ben Thompson

Although many believe that IoT might be over-hyped, I would assert the opposite; we are just starting to realize the enormous potential of a fully connected and digitally enabled world. For example:

- $1.7 trillion of value will be added to the global economy by the IoT in 2019. (source: Business Insider)
- 82% of enterprise decision makers say that the IoT is strategic to their enterprise. (source: IDC)
- Although exabytes of IoT data are generated every day, 88% of it remains unused. (source: IBM Research)

Despite this obvious opportunity, most enterprises are limited by the costs and time lag associated with transmitting data for analysis. To compound the problem, data streams from IoT devices are complex, and there is little ability to reuse analytical programs.

Shock 1: The market is undergoing a digital transformation: we are on our way to 5 billion smartphones globally, impacting all types of commerce and customer/supplier engagement. The overall connected device growth is even greater, and is accompanied by a data explosion.

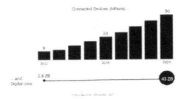

This changes the nature of customer/supplier and stakeholder engagement, rendering many traditional forms of distribution and communication economically unviable. Every business process will change over the next 5 years. A few companies will lead this digital transformation, but others will simply follow or ignore it at their peril. Perhaps the best example of this digital transformation at the intersection of devices and data is DocuSign. This company has digitally enabled two of the most common processes in an enterprise: signatures and transaction management (contracts and signed documents). Not only have they taken these traditionally paper-based and lengthy processes and reduced the number of steps, they have enabled any endpoint device to be part of the workflow. What once took a digital office and 5 paper-based steps now requires a quick electronic workflow, which can be executed from any device. This is digital transformation at the intersection of data and devices, and is something that can be applied in countless industries and business processes.

Chapter 2: Stakeholders and Distribution

"In the old world, you devoted 30% of your time to building a great service and 70% of your time to shouting about it. In the new world, that inverts. If I build a great product or service, my customers will tell each other." –Jeff Bezos

Products and services must be built with a "usage first" mindset. Clients and users need to be attracted to products by their experiences with those products. Clients should be begging for more because they are so delighted with their experiences and outcomes. If you build great products, clients will tell each other about them. The best way to make a product available for usage is through demos, freemium versions, downloads, and easy access via the cloud.

Many organizations spend most of their time focused internally. Some take a break from that and think about clients, which is great. But clients are only one of the three stakeholders that should drive thinking and behavior. Product development organizations live or die by how they treat, communicate with, and interact with their constituents, which are equally important:

- *Clients* include the company itself and the teams and organizations that make up the company.
- *Developers* include the builders within the company, who are focused on innovation.
- *Users* include the individual consumers of a product or service that is delivered by the company.

How do you make it easy for each constituent to work with you and your products or services? The organization should obsess over answering that question. With each new product idea, you need to be able to articulate the "must have" experience and the target of that experience (clients, developers, or users) before debating how and why a product or feature would be useful. This requires a rigorous process for identifying the most passionate stakeholders and getting their unstructured feedback.

Shock 2: Users in the consumer world and in the business world have changed. As Chamath Palihapitiya once said, "the business model of the future is to serve individuals." The internet is democratizing traditional incumbent advantages. Every incumbent in any industry has traditional distribution models and methods of customer/supplier interaction. The change in users and the aforementioned digital transformation is eroding these legacy advantages. Here are some sample models from select industries:

Industry	Traditional Model		New Model
Enterprise software	Face-to-face sales and resell partners		Digital try/buy
Healthcare/Pharma.	Face-to-face sales and wholesalers		TBD
Agriculture	Dealer/distributor networks		Direct and digital
Retailers	Storefronts		Direct delivery

The stakeholders have changed. For nearly every company, buyers and how they buy have changed. These changes make your traditional distribution model irrelevant, or at least less relevant. This shock forces any company to rethink its distribution strategy and to reassess who its real stakeholders will be. No matter what business you are in, there is a traditional model (yours) and there is a new model (sneaking up on you or not yet defined). Be sure to research, acknowledge, and understand the new model. Then chart a course. The best business model for the internet era is high volume and low price/cost per unit. This is not the world to which the non-tech elite is accustomed. Adapt, or be left behind.

Chapter 3: Data for Competitive Advantage

"If you want to receive something you've never had, you are going to have to do something you've never done." –Chuck Hodges

During the 20th century, scale effects in business were largely driven by breadth and distribution. A company with manufacturing operations around the world had an inherent cost and distribution advantage, leading to more competitive products. A retailer with a global base of stores had a distribution advantage that could not be matched by a smaller company. These scale effects drove competitive advantage for decades. As we have seen, the internet has changed all of that.

In the modern era, there are three predominant scale effects:
- *Network*: lock-in that is driven by a loyal network (Facebook, Twitter, Etsy, etc.)
- *Economies of Scale*: lower unit cost, driven by volume (Apple, TSMC, etc.)
- *Data*: superior machine learning and insight, driven from a dynamic volume of data

Shock 3: The price of computation has plummeted, enabling the fragmentation of industries on the basis of data and analytics. At the same time, the price of collecting and analyzing data has plummeted as well.

It used to be that a company interested in data and analytics would spend all of its available funds on the computation alone, or perhaps the compute and the data acquisition. This left little or nothing with which to build the algorithms and intellectual property that could drive meaningful learning and predictions. With the advent of cloud and big data, the economics have changed forever.

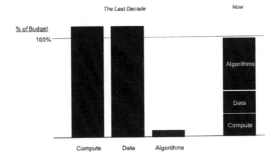

Data and compute have become relatively cheap, making more investment available for the development of algorithms and technology around that data.

For the first time, data has become a competitive weapon, creating a moat around an enterprise. For a company to transition to this era, it must be able to take advantage of this shift in economics and harness the power of analytics and machine learning. Machine learning on a large body of data is now as strong a competitive advantage as network effects or economies of scale. Anyone has access to cheap computational resources, so all that is needed is access to a meaningful (and ideally unique) data set.

Chapter 4: The Great Reskilling

"The secret of change is to focus all of your energy, not on fighting the old, but on building the new." –Socrates

In 2005, Geoffrey Moore published *Dealing with Darwin*, which offers a glimpse into how companies innovate during each phase of their evolution. Moore paints a picture of a business environment that is ever more competitive, globalized, deregulated and commoditized. Unsurprisingly, the combination of these forces puts immense pressure on companies to find ways of innovating in an increasingly complex environment.

Competition and innovation have been forever changed. But their effects on companies are merely the beginning. The next assault will be on individuals within companies. In the next five years, every employee will be dealing with Darwin personally. As Darwin famously said, "It is not the strongest of the species that survive, nor the most intelligent, but the ones most responsive to change." The great reskilling will be a test to identify the most adaptable individuals.

Individuals first dealt with Darwin on substantial levels during the Industrial Revolution, continuing through the 1900's, when factories began replacing small traditional industries. As factories appeared, demand for labor heightened. But factory work was quite different from traditional work and quickly became known for its poor working conditions. Even worse, because most factory work did not require a particular strength or skill, workers were considered unskilled and easily replaceable. At first, factory workers were replaced by other workers, but eventually they were automated away.

Economists typically categorize three kinds of work in a country: agriculture (farming), industry (manufacturing), and services. Each type of work plays a role in the economy, but macroeconomic forces have changed the mix over time. As you can see in the following figure, although 70 percent of the labor force worked in agriculture in 1840, the agricultural share reduced to 40 percent by 1900 and today sits at a mere 2 percent. Such shifts force employees to adapt and to experience Darwin on a personal level.

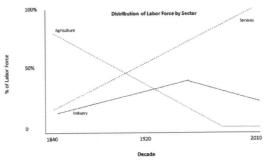

Source: https://www.minnpost.com/macro-micro-minnesota/2012/02/history-lessons-understanding-decline-manufacturing

These shifts have accelerated in the past 15 years, a period during which productivity has exploded, and struck at traditional workers and approaches. Thanks to widespread automation, broad acceptance of best practices and experience, skills that were once valued—and, indeed, that were necessary for industry—have been reduced to commodity services. Could the same thing happen to traditional information technology (IT) jobs?

The cloud has profoundly affected IT. Although moving to the cloud can reduce the costs of starting a company and can help cut capital expenses, the cloud's bigger impact will be on the traditional definition of a skilled IT worker. As organizations move to the cloud, the importance of traditional IT roles and skills—systems administrator, architect, database administrator, IT operations—will diminish, or even be eliminated over the next 5 to 10 years. Make no mistake: this shift will take a long time to play out. But now is the time to prepare for the coming revolution.

Shock 4: Companies no longer have the skills they need to make the transition. The skills for success in many professions and industries are changing. A company that used to have an army of IT specialists to run systems, now needs an army of data scientists. A company that prided itself on merchandising, now needs algorithms. When every business process is digitized or "datafied", the skill requirements of a business change fundamentally. *We are on the cusp of a great reskilling in the mature economies of the world.*

Imagine an organization with revenue of $1 billion, and assume that it spends 6 percent of its revenue per year on IT. With those assumptions, the company dynamics probably look like this:

	Today
Revenue	$1 billion
IT Budget (6%)	$60 million
PY Rate	$200,000
# of IT Employees	300
% of work in Cloud	0%

For such a company, the decision to shift to the cloud will be predicated on increasing leverage and efficiency, and will force a rethinking of the workforce. There is good news— salaries of employees will go up as they acquire rare and sophisticated skills—but there is also a negative: traditional IT skills will be less in demand, because much of that work will have been automated by the shift to the cloud.

	Today	Tomorrow
Revenue	$1 billion	$1.2 billion
IT Budget (6%)	$60 million	$50 million
PY Rate	$200,000	$250,000
# of IT Employees	300	200
% of work in Cloud	0%	50%

This shift represents both a pitfall and an opportunity for individuals. Indeed, the greatest risk lies in doing nothing—in merely continuing business as usual. More tools and education are available than ever before for individuals who decide that they want to be leaders in the data era. Data science will be the data era's defining skill. Though traditional IT skills will remain important for som, such skills will be increasingly less relevant in the cloud-centric data era.

Part II: 7 VITAL SIGNS OF A POST-TECH WORLD

In 2015, General Stanley McChrystal published Team of Teams: New Rules of Engagement for a Complex World. It was the culmination of his experience in adapting to a world that had changed faster than the organization that he was responsible to lead. When he assumed command of the Joint Special Operations Task Force in 2003, he recognized that their typical approaches to communication were failing. The enemy was a decentralized network that could move quickly and, accordingly, none of his organization's traditional advantages (equipment, training, etc.) mattered.

He saw the need to reorganize his force as a network, combining transparent communication with decentralized decision-making authority. Said another way, decisions should be made at the lowest level possible, as quickly as possible, and then, and *only* then, should data flow back to a centralized point. Information silos were torn down and data flowed faster, as the organization became flatter and more flexible.

Observing that the world is changing faster than ever, McChrystal recognized that the endpoints were most valuable and where most decision making should take place. This prompted the question:

What if you could combine the adaptability, agility, and cohesion of a small team with the power and resources of a giant organization?

Many organizations around the world have a similar problem: *data, information, and talent are locked into an antiquated and centralized model.* The impact is that professionals in most organizations do not have the data that they need or the autonomy to act, in the moment that it is required, to make the optimal decision.

Adapting and leading a company to success in the post-tech era requires as much business, operations, and financial skill, as it does technology skill. This is not just an IT initiative or the roll-out of new business applications; this is an acceptance of the idea that this is The End of Tech Companies, and accepting technology as the basis for competition. All companies that decide to embrace this technology imperative must start by assessing their vital signs. These are the seven vital signs for a post-tech world:

- Capital allocation
- Product strategy
- Design thinking
- Go-to-market strategy
- Work habits and tools
- Talent
- Instrumentation

These vital signs will determine a company's existence in the post-tech world. Although each vital sign might be slightly different based on the industry, unit economics, and business model, they are generally applicable to every business.

Chapter 5: Capital

"Diversification is protection against ignorance. It makes little sense if you know what you are doing." –Warren Buffett

A company cannot make the transition to the new era without a dramatic change in capital structure and how dollars are spent. Just think about it: a company's capital structure and spending were geared for a business model that was successful in the last decade, not the next decade. The sales and marketing expenses in most companies, tied up in traditional distribution channels, force an under-investment in technology, product innovation, and digital engagement. This is a death spiral for those seeking business leadership in the next decade.

Every company must rethink its relative spending on product development, sales, marketing, and G&A. It will be different than the mix that facilitated (or didn't facilitate) market leadership in the past. Let's use pure-play software companies as an example:

Company Type	Sales & Marketing % of Revenue	R&D % of Revenue	All Else/ Profits
High Growth Software Company	50%	30%	20%
Mature Software Company	20%	13%	67%
The Inverted Enterprise	20%	40%	40%

In the software industry, spending is remarkably consistent across enterprises at a similar stage in their life cycle. For example, look at the R&D spending of three large technology companies as a percentage of product revenue:

Microsoft	~13%
Google	~13%
Oracle	~13%

Although the absolute numbers vary, the relative spending is consistent. It is similar in higher growth software companies as well, where they tend to spend more on R&D as a percentage of revenue (30%+) and more on Sales & Marketing (~50%). Again, consistent. *But, maintaining a capital allocation structure (and overall capital structure) that mirrors your competition is not a leadership strategy.* The leaders will develop a unique point of view on how to rework their spending and use that to create a new business model. The best example is what I call the "inverted enterprise".

The inverted enterprise inverts the traditional allocation of capital between Sales & Marketing, R&D, and everything else as a percentage of revenue. One of the best examples of an inverted enterprise today is Atlassian, a company founded in 2002 that went public in 2015. Atlassian built its business model on digital distribution, foregoing the traditional costs of scaling an enterprise software company. Instead of selling to enterprises (CIO's, etc.), they decided to sell directly to users. They focused on new users in the market (developers), turning Shock #2 into a strength. This left them with more capital for innovation, along with compensation and pay equity, to hire the best engineers to drive that innovation.

Most companies that buy into the idea of modernizing their capital structure overlook the need to reallocate spending towards compensation and equity for employees. Without that foresight, the war to acquire talent (one of the seven vital signs), is all but lost.

Chapter 6: Product Strategy

"Deciding what not to do, is as important as deciding what to do." –Steve Jobs

One of the most common refrains in every organization today is, "We don't have enough resources." Or, "We know what to do, but don't have the time or money." **This is a choice, not an issue.** If something does not have the right resourcing, it is because the organization is choosing that. The issue is typically resourcefulness, not resources. A company cannot lead in innovation without dedicating resources to explore and try things that, by definition, are likely to fail. Identifying the important waves to ride is important. It is equally important to actually ride those important waves (i.e., to execute on them).

It is well documented that mature companies struggle to innovate. Some point to "The Innovators Dilemma", some point to culture, and conventional wisdom often says that they do not have the right talent. Each of these interpretations is overly simplistic. There are three reasons why mature companies struggle to innovate:

- *A company tries to invest in technology that has natural synergy with its existing products instead of investing to disrupt what already exists or investing in unrelated opportunity areas.* Generally speaking, it is unlikely that exponential growth areas will be synergistic or complementary to the existing portfolio.

- *A company is more focused on what the competition is doing instead of what clients or users need.* There is a *huge* difference between obsessing over clients and obsessing over the competition. When you do the latter, by definition you are already behind. *Innovation comes from a thoughtful understanding of how to solve a pressing issue for a client.*

- *A company bets on concepts, proposals, or ideas, instead of on people and teams.* The latter requires management flexibility to trust that the team will figure it out, even if "it" changes dramatically over time. Innovators bet on people. And betting on people does not fit into a large company management system.

There is a way to change the culture towards organic innovation. "Product Horizons", a portfolio strategy, has been around for years, but it is still relevant. The traditional model for product horizons is captured here:

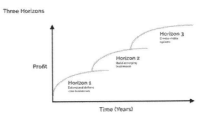

Given the current pace of change in the market and the macroshocks discussed previously, a product strategy requires an expanded and refined view of this horizons model. In short:

- There should be a Horizon 0.
- The definition of each horizon should evolve slightly.
- Capital allocation between horizons must be intentional and aggressive.

Horizon 0	Horizon 1	Horizon 2	Horizon 3
30% of Revenue 5% of R&D Majority Outsourced	58% of Revenue 15% of R&D	20% of Revenue 70% of R&D	2% of Revenue 10% of R&D
Product A	Product F	Product L	Product U
Product B	Product G	Product M	Product V
Product C	Product H	Product N	Product W
Product D	Product I	Product O	Product X
Product E	Product J	Product P	
	Product K	Product Q	
		Product R	
		Product S	
		Product T	

Horizon 0

These are products that will be outsourced or discontinued, so that you can spend the majority of your investment in Horizons 2-3. This is not easy. In fact, these are the hardest decisions you will have to make across your vital signs. But it is not optional. Every company must be selective in its investment allocation across products and product life cycles.

Horizon 1

This represents the majority of the company revenue today, but the R&D costs must be reduced to a mere 15% of the total budget to ensure that the company is investing for the future. For the most part, these products will remain in-house, but the pace of innovation will slow down.

Horizon 2

This is the new growth engine for the next 6-24 months. Aggressively invest here to drive the growth that is needed in that time frame. As these products mature, they move to Horizon 1. The majority of a company's R&D investment (70%) should be here.

Horizon 3

These are the big, risky bets that are likely to fail. But if you do not do anything on this fringe, the company's chances for break-out innovation are minimal. It is a lottery ticket, but with the right team, your numbers might come up.

After the product or service offerings are grouped by horizon, choose your "lead-with" offerings for marketing, PR, and digital exposure. With traditional distribution channels not as relevant, it is not practical to feature all of the company's products. Each company must choose the concise set of products or services that will represent the company. Others will continue to be sold, but these are the 1-3 products or services that will be aggressively marketed, both through traditional means and digitally.

These focus products or services must come from Horizon 2, because this is near-term innovation that clients or users can utilize for value now. If a company markets Horizon 3 products, credibility is lost, a classic example of vaporware.

Product strategy does not come easily to most companies. It tends to get wrapped up in company politics, personal preferences, and the human desire to please existing clients. However, in every case, if these are the driving forces, the company will fail at innovation and the products will atrophy. These are perhaps the most important decisions that a company will make, so be careful how far down they are delegated. Product strategy and investment decisions should be made by the person who is ultimately accountable for delivering product revenue.

Chapter 7: Design Thinking

"There is no such thing as a commodity product, just commodity thinking." –David Townsend

Anthony DiNatale was born in South Boston. He entered the flooring business with his father in 1921 and began a career of craftsmanship and woodworking. In 1933, he founded DiNatale Flooring in Charlestown, working job to job, primarily in the northeast United States. In 1946, Walter Brown approached DiNatale and asked him to build a floor for a new basketball team to use. DiNatale quoted him $11,000 to complete the project, and a deal was struck.

DiNatale quickly went to work, knowing that he had to be cost-conscious because he had bid aggressively to win the project. He gathered wood from a World War II army barracks and started building. But then he noticed a problem: the wood scraps were too short for his traditional approach to building a floor. So he began to create an alternating pattern, changing the direction of the wood pieces when fastening them together. He kept creating 5-foot panels, and when he had 247 of them, his work was complete.

Walter Brown was owner of the Boston Celtics. When the Celtics moved into the Boston Garden in 1952, the floor that had been commissioned by Brown in the year of their founding went with them. The floor was connected by 988 bolts and served as the playing surface for 16 NBA championships between 1957 and 1986.

DiNatale was a craftsman, an artist, a woodworker, but most prominently a designer. He made use of what he had and designed what would become the iconic playing surface in professional sports. The floor became a home-court advantage for the Celtics, because competitors complained about its dead spots and intricacies.

Design is enduring. Design is timeless. And, every once in a while, design becomes a major advantage.

The End of Tech Companies is forcing each company in every industry to rethink its definition of skilled workers, its investments, and its growth strategy. Design is essential for companies that want to prosper in this new environment.

According to the KPCB report *Design in Tech 2016*, since 2004, 42 design firms have been acquired by the technology sector. More importantly, ~50% of those acquisitions occurred last year, with companies like IBM, Accenture, Google, and Facebook being the most active buyers. Is this a fad, or a recognition that user expectations have changed?

Design is about tapping into how people feel when they use your product. Do they find it shockingly simple, yet highly functional, leading to an "ah-ha" moment? They should. It has been said that people don't buy products; they buy better versions of themselves. When you're trying to win customers, are you listing the attributes of a product or can you vividly describe how it will improve their lives? Users will be attracted to the latter.

John McCabe, the coordinator of user experience (UX) design at Savannah College of Art & Design (SCAD), says it best:

"Interaction, interactive, industrial, service, and graphic design all have core aspects that are found in UX design. They all understand human factors—psychology—they understand how people are going to go through a space. To me, I really feel that UX is definitely foundational for all design."

Whether you make software or hard goods, there is a single, ultimate test of design and your product strategy: is your product available for download or purchase on your website and can any target user easily get started? For the vast majority of companies in any industry, the answer is "no". Many of them say that this approach does not apply to them. It *does*. And it is not enough to have a downloadable whitepaper or demo. A user or a client must be able to experience an engagement with your company without talking to a single person. This is the ultimate simple test.

I once asked my team at IBM to think about a great product or service that they used in their lives and to share the feelings that came to mind. Here is a sampling of what I heard: "Value." "Changed my life." "No effort." "Amazing." "Just works." "Awesome." "Intuitive."

If you are at a company where the products and services do not evoke similar feelings, the company is in trouble. It might not be obvious yet, but time will be cruel.

Products in every industry begin with design and also with the user. However, unlike in the past, we can no longer assume that the user is also a buyer, a customer, a middleman, or a distributor. Today people frequently use a product without ever having established a relationship with the company that made it. That requires a significant change in thinking. A company cannot modernize product offerings without a design team. So hiring a design team (by using money that has been freed up from capital reallocation) is step one.

Doing design right is hard, and there are plenty of false designers and false approaches. Some companies have engineers posing as designers or marketing leaders claiming design experience. You would not hire an engineer who had only studied outside of the engineering field, so why do that with design? Hire students from the best design schools who have committed their lives to creativity.

The catch is that they will not fit into your company culture. Accept that. The company culture is not able to design great products, which is exactly why it must change. A great design team will be picky and discerning. It will want to do deep user research. Designers will work at different paces. They will ask questions that drive the engineering team crazy. This is exactly what the company needs.

Great product teams obsess over clients, extract what they hear into market-level requirements, and consistently wow both new and existing clients. And they have a process for reviewing what they have learned from clients, every week, without fail. This disciplined obsessing over what is heard, comparing notes with others, discussing, hypothesizing, and then repeating, becomes an enduring approach to ensuring that they are building the right things. The company will start to demonstrate a shared mindset between design, product management, and development. Only then will you know that the investment in design is starting to pay off.

Any company can improve in the area of deciding what to build and understanding why. But it requires three non-negotiable decisions:

- Build a world-class design team with professionals trained in design, and support them as they disrupt the culture.

- Define a process to ensure that client feedback, not just from existing clients, is at the center of all efforts. (This is how Slack grew so fast, as detailed in this *First Round Review* article.) Ideally, you want this to be your culture, not a process. But sometimes you need a process to facilitate the culture shift.

- Create a framework for thinking about all the dimensions of a product. IBM's 6 Universal Experiences is a great example of this, but there are others.

Design has risen to the forefront in all industries because customer expectations around products have changed. It is no longer simply about how a product or service is used, it is about the overall experience of finding it, trying it, using it, and (perhaps) getting assistance with the product or service. IBM calls this the <u>Six Universal Experiences</u>, and this approach applies to nearly any product or service in any industry. The six universal experiences are:

- Discover, try, and buy
- Get started
- Everyday use
- Manage and upgrade
- Leverage and extend
- Get support

Most companies think only about everyday use, but true design requires a broader perspective. Each experience offers opportunities to solve unmet needs and emotionally bond users to products.

Discover, try, and buy
Make it easy for users to find your product or service. Demonstrate, do not explain. Offer an easy transition from "try" to "buy".

Get started
Avoid the need for manuals or documentation. Any targeted user should be able to engage immediately.

Everyday use
Make using the product or service a joy. Provide value in every interaction.

Manage and upgrade
Make improvements easily available, in an elegant way that increases the user's joy and engagement.

Leverage and extend
Make it easy to augment every product or service by connecting to an ecosystem of partners or jobs to be done.

Get support

Support users according to their preferences, be that through text, chat, Facebook, etc. Make support a delightful experience that doesn't repel users.

Companies can implement all of these suggestions, yet still fail in design. In fact, many organizations do. Success comes down to how well the design team is integrated into the company culture: is design viewed as a "service bureau," or does design have a seat at the executive table? This is the most critical aspect of design thinking within any organization.

To be taken seriously and not be treated as a service bureau, design must be at the same level as other key reporting functions in the organization, whether it is HR, Legal, Marketing, or Finance. All of these functions play a key role and almost always report to the CEO or a senior leader; design must be the same. For design to truly fulfill its role, it needs the same voice and visibility.

If an organization is all about the experience, usability, and a "wow" factor, then design is critical for driving those values. Look at the industries and companies that are known for elegant design: fashion, Apple, Samsung, Porsche, Mercedes, etc. In each case, design has a seat at the table. In some cases, design is at the head of the table.

Chapter 8: Go-to-Market Strategy

*"Without strategy, operations and tactics are incoherent." –
Ramo*

Consistent with the horizons work de in Chapter 6 ("Product
Strategy"), the first go-to-market change is the hardest: stop
selling all the products that you have. This is counter-intuitive.
Most mature companies have too many products. They've
grown over the years through organic innovation and
acquisitions, largely driven by customer demands. This
product sprawl is rarely rationalized, and decisions to
discontinue products are rare. Even worse, many products are
sustained because of a handful of paying customers. This is a
death spiral that virtually ensures that the company will not
grow. A good product strategy (described in Chapter 6) can fix
this problem, but changing a product strategy takes time, and
the company must sell something now. How do you deal with
that?

The company must choose a handful of lead-with products,
ideally the same ones that were chosen as the lead-with digital
offerings described in Chapter 6. With that decision made, all
channels-to-market (digital, inside sales, face-to-face,
partners) can convene around a single message. It is shocking
how few mature companies are able to do this. Having grown
through acquisition and expanded their product or service
offerings over time, most companies never want to stop
anything and focus on the handful of things that are
working. And rarely do they want to alter their marketing
message to something broader, such as an integrated suite or
a platform. This is a missed opportunity.

The economics of platform business models are proving
superior in the internet era. The ability to align the interests of
your customers, suppliers, partners, and stakeholders around
a single platform strategy can deliver exponential growth. Let's
look at a sampling of companies with market capitalizations

over $50 billion who have embraced technology as being fundamental to their business:

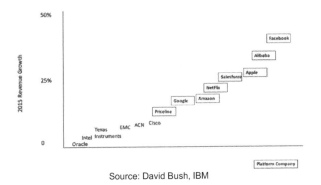

Source: David Bush, IBM

Each company that is designated as a platform company has centered its customer engagement on a single product or platform. Therefore, all of the strength of its go-to-market investment (in advertising, marketing, and sales force) is tightly aligned. It is no coincidence that the growth of these companies is outstripping their multi-product obsessed counterparts.

A company cannot be successful without a singular and simple go-to-market message supported by no more than 1-3 offerings. There was a time when this was not true, in the days of face-to-face sales, when customers had to be educated by a salesperson. The salesperson could wade through the complexity of a large product catalog and make recommendations to the customer. Unfortunately (or fortunately), those times are past. The internet has democratized product education and research, in many cases obviating the need for a direct salesperson.

In 1961, Alan Shepard was the first American launched into space. He traveled aboard the Redstone rocket, which was a rocket program that had been born out of the military at the close of World War II. As Shepard sat aboard the Redstone rocket, about to take off, he had the realization that he was sitting aboard a bunch of assembled parts, each of which was provided by the lowest bidder. This did not bring him great comfort for his journey.

Shepard recounts that when the rocket took off, the noise of the flight was unbelievable, and that the vibration was so dramatic that he could not even read the instruments. As he joggled along, unable to read anything and seeing only the blur of the dials, faith alone kept him from aborting the mission. The vibrations, which were not unexpected, were caused by resistance from the air outside, as Shepard plowed his way into space. The sound and the vibration increased to the point where he was convinced that the aircraft would fall apart until...BOOM! He was now supersonic and entered space, a completely silent flight. It was the most beautiful thing that he had ever experienced, immediately following the roughest moments of his life. The lesson that he derived from this experience is to hang on when things are toughest, because the most beautiful experience might be just around the corner.

That is what it feels like to change your go-to-market strategy. Extreme resistance, fear, and then...BOOM! An aligned organization, focused on a single message. To achieve this, an organization must have the courage to identify the winners and losers in its own product catalog.

Chapter 9: Work Habits and Tools

"Every single process in the company (compensation, measurements, etc.) is built for the old strategy." –Lou Gerstner

It has been said that "process transformation in a company is like setting your hair on fire and putting it out with a hammer." The Lou Gerstner quote captures that sentiment best, by articulating the fact that there is nothing wrong with the current work habits, tools, and processes, except that they all have to change, given the new strategy. He went on to say that successful companies suffer from a success syndrome: they find out what made them great and build processes to make it repeatable. But then the world changes.

Speed drives exponential improvements and outcomes in any organization. If you complete a task in one hour instead of one day, your mean time to a positive outcome is 500% faster. In product development, accelerating cycle times is an underestimated force in determining winners and losers. In sales, it is no different. Marketing is the same.

Pixar has a company principle that states, "We start from the presumption that our people are talented and want to contribute. We accept that, without meaning to, our company is stifling that talent in myriad unseen ways. Finally, we try to identify those impediments and fix them." Every product or service organization has to break down its own barriers to achieve its potential.

An organization cannot evolve to become a leader in the post-tech world unless the work habits and tools that are used to perform key operations change. Work habits are difficult to change, so change must begin with something tangible and impactful. It can start small through the adoption of new forms of communication (Slack, for example) or file sharing (Box,

Dropbox, etc.), but it must evolve to a completely new way of working. Think about how many companies have wired their thinking to believe that the creation of a PowerPoint presentation is "work". It is not. PowerPoint is just a means of communicating a story or information, which could just as easily be communicated through a real-time dashboard via Watson Analytics or a similar capability. A commitment to change work habits and tools can be simplified into three key points:

1. Reduce or eliminate traditional forms of communication (PowerPoint presentations, email, static BI reports).
2. Introduce new forms of collaboration and make them mandatory (file sync/share, persistent chat, social networking, GitHub for developers, video conferencing, and remote collaboration).
3. Ensure that the company's leaders become the first adopters of the new tools.

This is not an incremental change. A leader must be willing to completely abandon existing processes and tools. The impact will be quick and enormously positive. And the employees who do not like it might leave. That too will be a positive.

Try an experiment with email: if you send fewer emails, you will receive fewer emails. If you send no emails, you'll eventually stop receiving emails. Instead, transition your communications to a more productive medium (blogging, Slack, Skype, etc.). The options are limitless, but the changes in tooling will change the interactions.

It is easy to change tools; it just requires conviction and courage. It is much harder to change work habits. Countless organizations have adopted agile methods, yet they still have all the same meetings and conference calls and status reports. This means that they have adopted agile nomenclature, but not the practices and habits. Here are four suggestions for changing work habits and becoming more effective:

1. Conduct a calendar audit once a month. Document how time is being spent and the return on that time. Are you being busy or productive? A deeper version of this would be to track your time for a week. How much time do you spend reading and learning vs. sitting in meetings and talking?

2. Adopt the Rockefeller Habits: priorities, data, and rhythm.
    a. *Priorities*: Every team or organization should have a clear set of priorities that should be written down and shared at the start of most gatherings.
    b. *Data*: Identify the data that will be used to assess progress against the priorities. With everyone committed to the priorities, the data will show whether progress is being made.
    c. *Rhythm*: Commit to a daily rhythm of work and meetings (if necessary). Be intentional and be consistent.

3. Build a visual backlog of work to be done by your team or organization. Physically show work moving from the backlog to work-in-process to completed. Energize the team to focus on the outcome and the measurable impact of working the backlog. One of the greatest deterrents to productivity is constantly being caught in a reactive state. This approach is proactive, not reactive.

4. Commit to a daily stand-up. This is not a meeting. This is literally a stand-up, in which each team member talks about what they are focused on for that day. The stand-up should aim to be 15 minutes long, but certainly no longer than 30 minutes. This creates

mutual awareness and ensures an aligned effort toward the priorities and backlog.

Of all the recommendations in this book, the suggestions in this chapter might be the most difficult to adopt, because they require changing a set of habits. As Dominic Price from Atlassian says, "Tools are worthless without the right people, principles, and practices in place." There are many dimensions to changing work habits and tools. Change also requires the painful admission that other companies and colleagues might be more productive and effective than your team. Nevertheless, is necessary for survival.

Chapter 10: Talent

"Life is like a ten-speed bicycle. Most of us have gears we never use." –Charles Schulz

The expertise of an organization must advance faster than the rate of change that the organization desires. This means that the talent must change. And it is not a 10% change. It is closer to an 80% change. There are two ways to get there: hiring and training. For most companies, 50% of the workforce should be trained and retrained, and 50% probably needs to be refreshed with new talent from the outside. No one said this is easy. But, as discussed in Chapter 9, the ultimate goal is changing work habits to drive productivity. That means transforming the human capital.

Mandatory training does not work. If people have to be coerced into learning, they will not be able to make the necessary shift. If training is to have the desired impact, employees must have the desire and motivation to learn.

This excerpt from Jim Rogers in *Fortune* magazine captures it well:

> *The best advice I ever got was on an airplane. It was in my early days on Wall Street. I was flying to Chicago, and I sat next to an older guy. Anyway, I remember him being an old guy, which means he may have been 40. He told me to read everything. If you get interested in a company and you read the annual report, he said, you will have done more than 98% of the people on Wall Street. And if you read the footnotes in the annual report, you will have done more than 100% of the people on Wall Street. I realized right away that if I just literally read a company's annual report and the notes, or better yet, two or three years of reports, that I would know much more than the others. Professional investors used to*

sort of be dazzled. Everyone seemed to think I was smart. I later realized that I had to do more than just that. I learned that I had to read the annual reports of those I am investing in and their competitors' annual reports, the trade journals, and everything that I could get my hands on. But I realized that most people don't bother even doing the basic homework. And if I did even more, I'd be so far ahead that I'd probably be able to find successful investments.

That is the definition of a growth mindset, a characteristic of people who seek out training instead of just responding to a mandatory order. This is why training and hiring are equally important; because they lack intrinsic motivation, some people are just not trainable.

It is the leaders' responsibility to do the following:

1. Provide a self-paced training platform.
2. Provide badges and recognition for those who make progress.
3. Develop a curriculum to ensure that the right skills are being emphasized.

After that, it is all about the individual. People have to ask themselves: Do I have the drive and passion to be the smartest person in the room on any topic, no matter who is in the room?

The hardest thing about hiring is that if your company is going through this transition, it is difficult to attract the type of people that you need, early in the transition. There are two ways to overcome this. First, you have to completely change your hiring process and approach, inclusive of compensation. The employees that you want are interested in leverage for their time and upside when they are successful. So bonuses and equity become important, even if you typically did not offer this type of compensation for new hires. (Note: This is why your capital structure has to change). Second, a modern and inspirational work environment is necessary to attract the people that you need. They don't want to work at your sprawling cubicle campus in the woods; they prefer a small office in an urban setting with modern furniture and tools.

All of the normal hiring suggestions apply: hire those with a bias for action, who possess a mixture of depth and breadth, and those with a growth mindset. Hopefully, this is ingrained in the hiring process already. A more impactful idea, and one that is rarely practiced, is to focus on hiring teams, not individuals. Assume that you need a five-person team for a new digital initiative. Instead of interviewing and hiring one by one, be clear that this will be a team hire and that the company is looking for the five people who can work best together rather than those who perform best as individuals. Ideally, five who have worked together in the past. The tone is established from the outset.

Talent, not technology, is the driver of companies that make a successful transition to the post-tech world. Not every company has to make the changes in training and hiring practices that are suggested in this chapter – just the ones that want to survive.

Chapter 11: Instrumentation

"Only when the tide goes out do you discover who's been swimming naked." –Warren Buffett

Every business process and corresponding metric must be instrumented. A real-time dashboard of the metrics that matter is the new management system in a modern enterprise. Few companies have this. A shift to this approach will reveal a number of inefficiencies, because traditional approaches (static business intelligence reports for example) were able to mask issues. After an organization plumbs the important processes and applications with the appropriate instrumentation, measurement against key performance indicators will be available instantly and as needed. This will change performance management for the better.

If an executive requesting a sales report or operations analysis kicks off a manual process for gathering data, the company is not instrumented. Less than 1% of companies are instrumented today according to this definition. The primary issue with this is the mean response time to a problem or an opportunity; it is way too slow. Every company needs to instrument the following items:

- Customer satisfaction
- Product or service delivery and effectiveness
- Sales pipeline
- User and influencer engagement

Why these four? They are all-encompassing. With these four items continuously instrumented, a real-time view exists of what the market thinks of the company, how this is leading to a revenue growth opportunity, the degree of effectiveness of product or service delivery, customer satisfaction levels, and problem resolution times. This is a comprehensive view of the things that determine success or failure of the business.

Customer satisfaction

Are you getting likes or dislikes from your users and clients? Relying on face-to-face meetings for this feedback is not scalable. Digital feedback *is* scalable, as are surveys. Surveys that are automatically triggered after an issue or engagement are even more valuable. This approach is regularly practiced by automotive service centers, but it is not widespread among commercial enterprises. Net Promoter Scores (NPS) are interesting, but they are not real-time data. Instrumentation is about real-time measurement, in the moment.

Product or service delivery and effectiveness

Instrumented technology should eliminate 80% of product management jobs over the next five years. A company does not need product managers to ask users what they think when users are voting through their activities with an instrumented product. Understand what users love, what they like, or what they refuse to use. And change the product immediately to align with that feedback. Introduce new products or capabilities slowly, 10 users at a time. After each group of users, change the product based on the instrumented feedback. By user 100, you will have a product or service that users love.

Sales pipeline

For most companies today, this is the most instrumented process. With the right discipline, most companies have a fairly immediate view into sales, sales progression, and sales pipeline. More advanced companies have turned this into predictive models for what they believe will happen based on historical metrics. This is an easy place to start with instrumentation and there is no excuse for not having it in place.

User and influencer engagement

Every company operates in an ecosystem. That ecosystem includes partners, suppliers, users, companies, competitors, and many other types. Some have greater influence than others, and some are simply louder than others. A company that has instrumented user and influence engagement can tell the difference and use that data to optimize community engagement.

There is a story of an experienced investment banker teaching a group of interns about the business. He is given 45 minutes to address the class, with the goal of teaching them everything that he has learned about investment banking. He says:

> *These are the important people in the world (as he draws black dots on the whiteboard). I don't know how many there are, but there are not that many. Now, these are the people's orbits (as he draws black circles). Inside these circles are the people they know, the deals they do, their ideas, etc. Pretty much everything important in the world happens inside these circles. This (as he points to the middle) is where I want to be. This is our strategy. Thank you.*

Having a finger on the pulse of an ecosystem provides a real-time view into how your product, service, message, or brand is being received in the market. It is the lifeblood of your business.

Implementing a strategy for instrumentation is not as simple as buying a tool, although technology and tools might play a key role. First, a company must develop a clear view of what to instrument and how. Even more importantly is understanding the "why". Instrumenting the wrong thing will be a huge distraction, so put maximum effort into this first step. Second, a company must automate the "what" and "how". This could be developed internally or bought commercially, if there is an obvious solution that meets the need (such as

Salesforce for sales pipeline, for example). Third, instill a culture of usage. Many companies instrument something but then never use it to run the business and make decisions. This happens more often than anyone would imagine. The culture of usage starts at the top.

PART III: MAKING THE SHIFT

Chapter 12: Focus on What is Working

"Big will not beat small anymore. It will be the fast beating the slow." –Rupert Murdoch

Winemaking is an art. Although technology has brought a lot of science to the process, ultimately the winemaker is an artist, constantly tinkering, adjusting, and optimizing for quality. If winemaking were purely science, anyone with money could buy a vineyard, wrap it with technology, and produce great wine. But they cannot. In fact, countless people have tried and failed.

Winemakers accept what the earth gives them each year, and adjust accordingly. If it is colder than expected, they adjust their process, and perhaps produce fewer barrels. But the barrels that they produce are of the right quality. If the soil is different than expected, they adjust, perhaps resulting in larger than expected production. They do not try to "fix" the soil, they adjust to the soil. Said another way, they focus on what is working, instead of what is not. If they were preoccupied with all the problems, they could never produce anything great.

There is a disease in the business world that is becoming more acute: it is the inclination to focus on what is not working. It is human nature to identify problems, solve those problems, and believe that it will lead to improved performance. But, is that truly the best use of finite resources?

During a recent visit to a large industrial company, this disease was in full view. Like any other company that builds real things, this company has many dimensions to its business: clients that buy the machines, suppliers of components, R&D, sales, marketing, information technology, etc. Tens of thousands of employees, in hundreds of countries; a highly complex operation, in a dynamic and changing industry. They are obsessed with the things that are not working.

Eighty percent of this company's time and attention is spent on supply chain problems, issues associated with operating in a diverse set of divisions, challenges around reducing IT costs, etc. *Their mental capacity is funneled into things that are not working.*

Compare this with a much younger and smaller startup and the contrast is stark. If something it not working, the startup moves onto the next thing. They understand that time and mental capacity, the only truly finite resources, are too valuable to spend on something that is not working. They get a better return on their time by focusing on the things that *are* working.

Does this mean that larger enterprises can ignore their problems? No. By definition, does a startup have more flexibility in what it can focus on? Yes. That being said, if you find yourself spending 80%+ of your time on things that are not working, your company is destined for mediocrity.

This mindset is essential when an organization starts to consider the seven vital signs for a post-tech world. It is easy to become preoccupied with the challenges and with what isn't working. Such preoccupation will not lead to a successful outcome. Let's re-examine each of the vital signs from this perspective:

1. *Capital allocation*: Declare a new capital structure goal after looking at spending as a percentage of revenue. Do not spend any time rationalizing why something

was done in the past. Focus on the new capital structure and how you get there.

2. *Product Strategy*: Force a "horizons" mapping of products and adjust spending in each horizon. Again, do not spend time trying to understand why certain products are not working or trying to fix that. Focus on allocations by horizon and increasing investments in the things that will work.

3. *Design Thinking*: Hire a great design leader and great designers. Do not spend any time trying to train designers; that is an example of focusing on something that is not working.

4. *Go-to-Market Strategy*: Pick lead-with offerings and focus all attention on these. The bet is that these will work and that the company needs conviction to see that through. This is a great example of focusing on what is working.

5. *Work Habits and Tools*: Turn off old tools and habits and shift to new ones. Spend little time on porting old information to the new tools. Start fresh. See whether the company truly cannot live without the old.

6. *Talent*: Quickly assess the employees that can be retrained. This is the most critical decision that is made on talent.

7. *Instrumentation*: Every company needs to instrument metrics around customer satisfaction, product or service delivery and effectiveness, the sales pipeline, and user or influencer engagement. Pick one and get started.

Chapter 13: Divide and Conquer

"If nothing changes, nothing changes." –Nick Donofrio

Jeff Immelt, the Chairman and CEO of General Electric, has managed the company through a difficult time period. He took the helm right after September 11, 2001, navigated through the financial crisis when GE could not place its commercial paper, and led the company to exit its large exposure to financial services. In a speech last year, Immelt asserted that when a business fails, you find some or all of the following four items:

- Complicated accountability
- Too much cost in the wrong places
- Excessive priorities
- Low market awareness

Dividing and conquering is about making an intentional decision about where to invest talent (cost in the right places), communicating clear priorities, and simplifying accountability. Sometimes this means separating the teams that are focused on the "cash cow" businesses from the new opportunities. One way to do this is to establish Disruption Teams (D-teams) that will make the shift needed to win in this new era.

The role of the D-teams is to disrupt from within. D-teams assess what the organization is working on, identify opportunities, rapidly assemble a new team, and disrupt. This type of competitive fire will make the whole company better. With a D-team, accountability is clear; there is one leader, with full autonomy, moving as fast as possible with a tightly integrated team. Because there is a single leader, priorities are not a problem. They are clear, limited, and focused for maximum impact. The team should be provided with enough investment, but not too much. Small teams are more effective. The *modus operandi* of the D-team is to experiment, fail, and adjust. This prevents any low market awareness from having a negative impact.

The challenge with D-teams or any type of split between "cash cows" and the new offerings is conflict management and the culture of fear that this type of division creates. Books like *The Innovators Dilemma* or *Zone to Win* advocate for this split, but they do not really get into conflict management and culture of fear obstacles: this is where theory ends and reality sets in.

A company must understand and manage potential conflicts that arise with a split in mission or the creation of D-teams. The separate teams that are created will have a bias towards targeting the same users or customers. This will exacerbate the conflict. The leadership team must be specific about the target markets and focus areas. Although there will naturally be some overlap, it should not be direct. Recall that a major reason for the division is to attack new markets, not to just serve existing ones.

Incentives are also critical. Some part of the incentive structure must visibly and financially reward teamwork and collaboration. A leader should put more time into the incentive structure than the organizational structure. That rarely happens.

A divide and conquer approach will also create a culture of fear. The immediate reaction from the team that is focused on the "cash cows" will be the feeling that they represent the past, and that they will not receive further investment or focus from the business. The only way to dispel this culture of fear is with actions, not words:

- Demonstrate continued investment in marketing and products.
- Allow skills to be remixed by bringing in new talent.
- Communicate the reinvestment focus to clients.

A stagnant organization produces stagnant results. The whole point of a divide and conquer strategy is to drive focus: focus on future offerings while continuing to focus on existing offerings, clients, and markets. The split focus must be accompanied by proof of investment in both parts, otherwise the culture of fear will paralyze the company.

Chapter 14: Bridge the Past

"If I had asked people what they wanted, they would have said faster horses." –Henry Ford

Whether or not Henry Ford actually said this is debatable. But the spirit of the statement certainly permeated Ford's approach to innovation. He was less concerned about what customers said they wanted, and much more focused on what he felt customers needed, whether they knew it or not. This forward-looking approach is at the heart of an innovative culture.

The first Ford Model T was introduced in 1908. Although other automobiles had been available for over a decade, this was the first car that the masses could afford. This is why most people remember the Model T and not the Model A, which was actually the first automobile produced by Ford. The Model A, first brought to market in 1903, was a 2-cylinder vehicle that was not affordable for all. A key learning point on innovation is that form, function, and price are often equally important.

Ford's reputation as an innovator was cemented by the 38 years of innovation that followed the Model A. Ford quickly ramped up to one million cars sold by 1915. The first Ford truck arrived in 1917 (it had a Model T engine), followed by an enhanced 8-cylinder Model A in 1932. Then came the Ford Mercury in 1938 and the Jeep in 1941. Thirty-eight years of innovation, never once looking back.

The product roadmap is an all too familiar chart seen across product development companies today. It does not matter whether it is hardware, software, machines, or even consumer packaged goods; everyone has a view of where the product is today and where it will go in the future. The challenge that most successful companies face, which is well documented by Clayton Christensen in *The Innovators Dilemma*, is the trade-off between sustaining innovation (enhancing or improving your current products) and investing to build transformative products that attack new opportunities. The former is easy, whereas the latter is technically difficult, not to mention fraught with inherent cultural challenges.

If Ford had been preoccupied with sustaining innovation, there would have been a horse (albeit a better horse) on his product roadmap chart circa 1903.

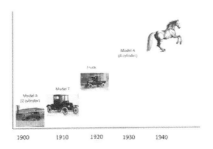

Because we all agree that this is ridiculous, why do so many companies fail at this task? Culture, inertia, existing client requests, existing skills, etc., are among the reasons. Next time that you are in a meeting where you see a team falling into this trap, just say "Take the horse off the chart!"

As "the horse is removed from the chart", an organization must put equal focus into building a bridge from the past to the future. In Ford's case, this was about demonstrating how the first automobile was an extension of the primary use case for a horse: transportation. The automobile eventually became more efficient but did not obviate the need for a horse in all cases. In other words, the automobile pointed to the future, but also needed to bridge the past by showing how it could be utilized for different purposes. Note: It would be another 20 years before modern machinery would show up on a farm.

"Bridging the past" has the following two elements:

- Acknowledgement that a company must "take the horse off the chart" and stop building the past. A quick glance at any company's product roadmap will quickly demonstrate whether or not this tenet has been embraced.
- Demonstration of a near-term future in which both products (past and future) are necessary.

With these two items in place, a company is well positioned to move towards the inevitable future.

PART IV: THE MAKER ERA

"We are defined by what we build. It's not just the engineering ambition that designed these structures, nor the 20 people who died building the Brooklyn Bridge. It's that we believe we can and decide to act." –Michael Lopp

In 1871, construction began to build a bridge over the Firth of Forth in Scotland. It was an essential project to connect a railway over the shortest possible route. The ever unpredictable weather in Scotland called for brick supports on top of the bedrock in the water.

The architect was Sir Thomas Bouch. When he was planning the design and construction of the bridge, he did extensive research on "wind loading", calculations designed to ensure that a structure will be able to withstand high winds. His research led him to the conclusion that extra wind loading was not needed. In addition, he made errors in assessing maintenance needs and quality control factors for the bridge. These oversights would prove costly in due time.

On December 28, 1879, a terrible storm appeared. Although the winds were reported as being very high (in excess of 60 mph), the bigger issue is that they were perpendicular to the bridge, putting maximum strain on the supports. The result became known as the Tay Bridge Disaster, as the bridge crumpled into the Firth, taking a rail car along with it.

Suffice it to say, it is now clear why the expression "botch a job" has persisted to this day. It is synonymous with an error in judgment leading to some sort of a miscue or disaster. Such is the life of a builder. As Dan Kaminsky once said, "If you build it, they will complain." The courage that it takes to put yourself out there as a builder or maker means that it is not something everyone will want to do. But there are signs that change is coming. The "Maker movement" is an essential aspect of surviving in the post-tech world.

Chapter 15: The Maker Era

"Developers make software for the world to use. The job of a developer is to crank out code – fresh code for new products, code fixes for maintenance, code for business logic, and code for supporting libraries." –Nick Hardiman

When was the last time you built something from nothing? Was it the time you had to make a diorama for a school project? How about a gift for someone else? Perhaps you composed a song for someone you love. Whatever it was, there is nothing quite like the feeling of creating something from nothing. It is a form of expression that invokes creativity, freedom, passion, and deep thinking. For these reasons, a growing number of people are inspired to learn new skills to make new things. Until recently, people who identified themselves as "makers" were considered hobbyists, do-it-yourselfers, craftsmen, or simply tinkerers. Although those makers are continuing to thrive, other makers in the form of Designers, Developers, Marketers, and the emerging Data Science Practitioners are moving out of niche areas into many professions across every industry. Some of these professions used to be considered Ivory Tower disciplines. But now, computer science, for example, has been penetrated by the "maker movement" and its practitioners simply recast as "developers".

Developers represent the largest maker movement of our time by making software for everything imaginable, from consumer applications to enterprise processes, to entire marketplaces and, most recently, to automated systems that can think. It is important to realize that these developer makers operate differently than others. For one thing, they are highly suspicious of "black box" solutions. Many vendors have tried to reach developer makers with proprietary software solutions, and failed. Developer makers also differ from other professions in how they work. For example, as Paul Graham states, "one reason programmers dislike meetings so much is that they're on a different type of schedule from other people.

Meetings cost them more." Although this was written about developers, it applies to any profession in which sustained attention is needed to build. He goes on to say that "when you are operating on a maker's schedule, meetings are a disaster. A single meeting can blow a whole afternoon, by breaking it into two pieces each too small to do anything hard in." Thinking gets shifted back to the fast-paced world of immediate actions and away from deep concentration. Reduce distractions, and developer makers become far more productive on account of their highly resourceful and self-reliant nature, providing highly detailed information about programs in the form of documentation, example code, and a thriving community. It is no wonder that developer makers are the makers who most significantly disrupt industries and professions. One profession that had been out of reach until recently is Information Management.

In early 2010, a diverse functional team sat down to discuss why user growth and revenue had slowed, even though installations were on the rise. Marketing professionals presented their campaign data that showed a strong conversion rate of web traffic to downloads. Product analysts showed that the free-to-paid conversion was steady. Lastly, financial analysts showed that the daily, weekly, and monthly active user counts were declining, along with subsequent revenue. Business analysts were on the hook to come up with an explanation for this disconnect. Unfortunately, they had neither access to data, nor a flexible data environment, nor the sophisticated analytical tools needed to connect the dots.

Meanwhile, the engineering team was collecting application log files, network delivery log files, installer log files, and license types as part of the quality control effort. These individuals were not considered part of the "information" or "business intelligence" group and therefore did not make this data available for others – until a group of data scientists and engineers, or data makers, convinced the engineering team to open its data assets to the organization through a distributed data environment built on Hadoop. As soon as these data makers were able to work with the data in an unrestricted way, they quickly developed data products, including curated data sets and business metrics, which could be validated by analysts before being rolled out to the rest of the organization. It took a team of data makers, who could facilitate a conversation across the two organizations, to expand the corpus of information that was available to the business. Data was programmatically used to solve the riddle of the user problem. As it turned out, the answer could be found in the combination of clickstream data, installer log files, and transaction records that showed a channel-specific relationship to specific product offerings that was not otherwise apparent.

As they disrupt the information consumption *status quo*, data makers are emerging as organizational change agents. Prior to 2011, Information Management consisted of a linear series of steps to produce a dashboard or report that could be distributed, perhaps quarterly, as part of a business review. Data makers apply creativity to attack business outcomes. They wrangle, munge, extract, and analyze data to transform it into a product that incites others to act. To foster a data maker culture, it is critical to make data available, provide an open forum for results to be discussed, and provide a collaborative environment for data artifacts to be shared across organizations.

Today these professions share information freely and promote education through workshops and online courses. Individuals and organizations are starting to realize that to do their best work or attract top talent, the walls between professionals must come down. Makers, by their very nature, are collaborative and open to all comers. Makers have driven the rise of open source software, meetups, hackathons, Massive Online Open Courses (MOOCs), and various programs that promote inclusivity in technology. This is the Maker Era; a key cultural condition for prospering in the post-tech world.

Chapter 16: Building a Maker Culture

"The key is not spending time, but in investing it." –Stephen Covey

Building a Maker culture is an investment, not an expense. It is a decision to invest in the creation of value that will form the basis of a company's success in The End of Tech Companies. Although many aspects of a Maker culture have permeated this book (tools, workspaces, investment shifts, etc.), one primary factor has not been discussed yet: time. A company cannot develop a Maker culture unless time and freedom are offered to those who can have the greatest impact.

The role of the leadership team in any company that wants to adapt to the post-tech world is to facilitate a Maker culture. Although there are many ways to do this, three approaches can drive short-to-long term results:

1. Create Maker time.
2. Provide internal seed funding.
3. Form D-teams.

Create Maker time

This approach is about recalibrating Maker workload, and perhaps was made most famous by Google's "20% time" approach, in which that company made it a policy that all developers could choose any topic to work on for 20% of their time. Although much has been written about this approach (for example, was the 20% supposed to be logged during nights or weekends?), the main point was being missed: Google was making a formal and visible declaration that Maker time is important. Any company can do this; it just takes courage and initiative. It might take time away from the "core" tasks of the engineering team, but this approach will pay off in the medium-to-long term.

Provide Internal Seed Funding

Launch an initiative whereby any Maker can bring forward an idea, build it out, and secure funding, much like a start-up would do. Empower anyone who has a vetted proposal to form a team, declare milestones, and make its development a full time job. If a team passes its first milestones, let them continue. Most companies will be shocked by the resulting innovation after they establish the right climate. This approach not only provides a method for systematic innovation, it also promotes employee retention. Great Makers love working on ideas about which they are passionate.

Form D-teams

This concept was first introduced in Chapter 13. A D-team is formed as a standalone unit to own an outcome from end to end. The team is self-contained, fully empowered, and mission focused. D-teams can be a seeding ground for a Maker culture, because members are driven by action and output. The collateral benefit of D-teams is that they create an energy and pressure that forces other teams to increase their output. Everyone wins.

A Maker culture is a necessary condition for any company to survive The End of Tech Companies. The three approaches introduced here are examples of how to foster the right environment. Different companies will adapt to the Maker era differently and must find approaches that work best for them.

Chapter 17: Build-Measure-Learn

"We are defined not by the technologies that we create but the process in which we create them." –Kelly Johnson

Every company will instinctively attempt to measure and manage the productivity of Makers, just like anything else. Attempts to instrument, measure, and manage Makers will ensure failure, and represents a fundamental mismatch between the culture that exists (top-down metrics) and the culture that needs to exist (bottom-up creativity). In some cases, a more iterative approach around build-measure-learn can also work, as demonstrated by a company that started this back in 1943.

The term "Skunk Works", which is used fairly frequently in the business world, typically describes a project that starts and runs "under the radar". The rationale is to make a small bet on some idea, away from the scrutiny of the executive team, to see if it can gain traction. But the real history behind Skunk Works is a bit more nuanced.

The term originated in 1943, when a Lockheed Martin employee, Clarence "Kelly" Johnson, received approval to start a secret project to build a jet fighter. The project was a huge success, completing in only 143 days, a pace that was unheard of at the time. Johnson's unconventional approach to organizing work and building the team was the real secret to their success. He codified his approach in 14 rules and practices, which can be found in great detail on Lockheed Martin's website. The spirit of those 14 practices includes the following items:

- Delegation of complete control; no dependencies
- Strong and small project offices
- Small teams
- Flexibility to make changes as you go
- Minimal status reporting

- Monthly cost reviews
- Specifications that are agreed to in advance
- Timely funding
- Strict control of outside influence or meddling
- Rewards that are tied to performance

These practices are very simple, which makes them timeless. But they are also difficult to implement in large and complex organizations. Over time, conventional wisdom has pared the Skunk Works idea down to the simple notions of "going dark" and "working under the radar". However, in reality, the spirit of Skunk Works is about simplicity of ownership and execution, coupled with a build-measure-learn philosophy of continuous improvement. This aligns well with the essence of a Maker culture.

Makers are not afraid of accountability, but they are afraid of bureaucracy. They are not afraid of short timelines, but they are afraid of regular reviews. Build-measure-learn, in the context of a Skunk Works team, can be a great way to empower the Makers in any organization.

EPILOGUE

"We are all faced with a series of great opportunities brilliantly disguised as impossible situations." –Charles Swindoll

Herman Melville wrote Moby Dick in 1851. It is a story about the whaling industry in the 19th century, capturing the intricacies of life at sea. In one part of the book, Melville describes a lantern that hangs from the ceiling in the Captain's quarter. No matter how rough the seas are, that lantern stays perpendicular to the center of the earth. The lantern with its inherent stability reveals the faults of everything around it. Leadership has to provide stability in the current era of uncertainty and disruption.

Danny Meyer, the increasingly well-known restaurateur (Gramercy Tavern, Union Square Cafe, and others), addresses the challenge of consistently communicating to his staff his expectations around standards of excellence. He mentions that many of the waiters and managers in his restaurants constantly test him as they push the limits of the standards in which he believes. Here is an excerpt from Meyer's book, *Setting the Table*:

"If you choose to get upset about this, you are missing the boat", Pat Cetta (Meyer's friend) noted. Pat pointed to the set table next to us. "First," he said, "I want you to take everything off that table except for the salt shaker. Go ahead! Get rid of the plates, the silverware, the napkins, even the pepper mill. I just want you to leave the salt shaker by itself in the middle." I did as he said, and he asked, "Where is the salt shaker now?"

"Right where you told me, in the center of the table."

"Are you sure that's where you want it?" I looked closely. The shaker was actually about a quarter inch off of center. "Go ahead. Put it where you really want it," he said. I moved it very

slightly to what looked to be smack-dab in the center. As soon as I removed my hand, Pat pushed the salt shaker three inches off center.

"Now put it back where you want it," he said. I returned it to dead center. This time he moved the shaker another six inches off center, asking again, "Now where do you want it?"

I slid it back. Then he explained his point. "Listen. Your staff and your guests are always moving your salt shaker off center. That's their job. It is the job of life. It is the law of entropy! Until you understand that, you're going to get pissed off every time someone moves the salt shaker off center. It is not your job to get upset. You just need to understand: that's what they do. Your job is just to move the shaker back each time and let them know exactly what you stand for. Let them know what excellence looks like to you."

Cetta is encouraging Meyer to provide the constant stability of the lantern on Melville's ship. And he is suggesting that Meyer accept the fact that there will always be instability around his attempts to do so.

Leaders have to know where their centers lie. They have to know it, talk about it, and never lose sight of it. The End of Tech Companies is upon us. Regardless of what industry you used to believe you were in, you are now being forced into the technology arena. Leading a company into this new environment requires the attributes that Danny Meyer learned about for his restaurant business: know where the center lies, talk about it, and never lose sight of it. A company will not make the transition to the post-tech era unless its leadership believes it in their gut. It is The End of Tech Companies, but it is a new beginning for your business.

ACKNOWLEDGEMENTS

David Schultz and David Townsend for advising on Chapter 7. Joel Horwitz for writing portions of Part IV and being an ambassador of a Maker culture.

Thanks to John Batelle and the team at NewCo Shift, for editing, encouragement, and distribution of portions of this book.

ABOUT THE AUTHOR

Rob Thomas is the General Manager of IBM Analytics.   He brings extensive experience in management, business development, and consulting in the high technology and financial services industries. He has worked extensively with global businesses and his background includes experience in business and operational strategy, high technology, acquisitions and divestitures, manufacturing operations, and product design and development.

IBM Analytics is IBM's flagship software division, providing software and technology to help clients and users make sense of their data. As the General Manager, Mr. Thomas has the business line responsibility and P&L ownership for the division.

Mr. Thomas' first book was Big Data Revolution, published by Wiley in 2015. *The Financial Times* called it "a case study of the philosophical assumptions that underpin the growing obsession with data." Mr. Thomas is an active writer on his blog (robdthomas.com) and is a frequent public speaker, featured at numerous business and industry events.

Mr. Thomas serves on the Board of Directors of the Domus Foundation.

He lives in New Canaan, CT, with his wife (Kristin) and three children.

ABOUT THE EDITOR

Roman B. Melnyk, Ph.D., is a senior member of the IBM
BigInsights Content Design team. Roman edited *Big Data
Beyond the Hype: A Guide to Conversations for Today's Data
Center*; *DB2 10.5 with BLU Acceleration: New Dynamic In-
Memory Analytics for the Era of Big Data*; *Harness the Power
of Big Data: The IBM Big Data Platform*; *Warp Speed, Time
Travel, Big Data, and More! DB2 10 for Linux, UNIX, and
Windows New Features*; and *Apache Derby - Off to the
Races*.

Roman co-authored *Hadoop for Dummies*; *DB2 Version 8:
The Official Guide*; *DB2: The Complete Reference*; *DB2
Fundamentals Certification for Dummies*; and *DB2 for
Dummies*.

ABOUT DOMUS

All proceeds from this book are being donated to Domus (http://domuskids.org/).

Our vision: No child shall be denied hope, love, or a fair chance in life.

Domus is a human services nonprofit which opened in 1972 and serves more than 1,100 of the most struggling youth in Stamford and New Haven, CT. Young people come to us with many challenges; most are living in abject poverty, have had involvement in the criminal justice system, and have experienced homelessness, neglect, abuse, academic failure, and chronic untreated healthcare issues. We do this through three primary service areas:

Educational: We operate two alternative charter schools in Stamford, Trailblazers Academy middle school and Stamford Academy high school, and a public school in New Haven, Domus Academy middle school, all serving students with significant academic and behavioral challenges. Family advocates help eliminate non-academic barriers to school attendance and success.

Community: We run the Chester Addison Community Center, the Trafigura Work & Learn Business Center, and four after-school enrichment programs.

Residential: We operate two group homes for homeless males who are wards of the State of Connecticut, as well as an independent living program.

In all of these programs, we deliver against our vision that no child shall be denied hope, love, or a fair chance in life.

Made in the USA
Middletown, DE
31 January 2017